YOGA

One Partner-Sharing & One Individual Yoga Class

HB
HINKLER BOOKS

Author: Lynley Woods
Art Director: Karen Moores
Editor: Jane Keighley
Graphic Artist: Melissa Carroll
Photographer: Glenn Weiss
Special thanks to models Sarah Burgess
and Matthew Dezoete-Baker

First published in 2005 by Hinkler Books Pty Ltd
17-23 Redwood Drive
Dingley, VIC 3172 Australia
www.hinklerbooks.com

Printed and bound in China

HINKLER BOOKS

ISBN 1 7415 7536 2

When practising yoga, always do the warm-up exercises before attempting any individual postures. It is recommended that you check with your doctor or healthcare professional before commencing any exercise regime. Whilst every care has been taken in the preparation of this material, the Publishers and their respective employees or agents will not accept responsibility for injury or damage occasioned to any person as a result of participation in the activities described in this book.

Contents

INTRODUCTION TO YOGA

Practising yoga can give the experience of lightness, release and joy. No-one is too young or too old to try it, because there are so many facets to this ancient, holistic life science. The word 'yoga' is derived from Sanskrit, one of the oldest known languages. It has a twofold meaning:

1 the verb, to bind or yoke, implying steady, consistent practise, and;

2 the noun, union, denoting the harmonising of all aspects of our being – body, mind and spirit.

The form of yoga with which most Westerners are familiar is hatha (the union of ha – the masculine sun and tha – the feminine moon). It's a unique blend of physical postures (asana), breath control (pranayama) and relaxation (or sense withdrawal – pratyahara).

Benefits

More than just a set of physical exercises, this combination promotes health, flexibility, strength, vitality, endurance and wellbeing on all levels – physical, emotional and mental. The physical benefits alone are a good incentive for practising yoga, which

- Strengthens, tones and revitalises your musculoskeletal system
- Cleanses, tones and maintains your vital organs, blood and lymph circulation
- Improves the functioning of your endocrine system, regulating the efficient production of hormones throughout your body

The control and co-ordination of your breath with the postures, along with the mental focus applied, gives the ability to stabilise and calm your mind and emotions, improving mental clarity and efficiency. People often find while practising yoga that they experience a cleansing effect, resulting in a feeling of lightness and an increase of energy. This can further inspire lifestyle changes including:

- An improvement in diet – reducing or eliminating refined and processed foods and replacing them with fresh, natural whole foods which increase the intake of life force (prana)
- Spending more time in fresh air and natural surroundings

Going Deeper

Even further, there can be the incentive for looking into the deeper levels of yoga. The ancient sages tell us that we are actually spiritual beings having a human experience for a short time on earth.

Our true essence is one of light and joy, and we can connect with that essence by taking some time to withdraw from our worldly concerns, allowing our mind to slow down and move into silence.

The realisation of our true nature and potential enables us to lead more enriching lives, and to feel happier and more complete. That state of inner-peace has a positive effect on our behaviour and ultimately our relationships with people, our community and the environment.

About Partner-Sharing & Individual Yoga

Partner-Sharing & Individual Yoga has three sections:

1 A general class.

2 An added section of partner-assisted postures.

3 A guided relaxation.

If you are new to yoga, there are gentler variations of the more difficult postures, allowing scope for progress. If you are familiar with it, *Partner-Sharing and Individual Yoga* can add variety to your practise.

Suggested Guidelines

1 Yoga is ideally practised slowly with body awareness and co-ordinated breathing.

2 Never force yourself into a position. Work to the best of your ability but relax. This will make the stretches easier and open your mind to experience the benefits. If you want to create a challenge, learn the difference between discomfort and pain. A little discomfort is fine in order to make progress. Strain or pain is the body's signal to back off.

3 Yoga stimulates the metabolism and enhances the effects of whatever is consumed. If taking prescribed medication (or you have ANY injuries or medical conditions) consult a medical practitioner first.

4 Postures are best practised on an empty stomach, so first thing in the morning is ideal. But find a time that suits your lifestyle, where you can be undisturbed and relaxed, in order to benefit from the centring effects of yoga.

5 Practise in a clean, airy space, one that preferably enhances feelings of wellbeing. You don't need a large area. If you don't have a yoga mat, a carpeted area or a non-slip rug will do. Keep a cushion and blanket close by in case you need them. Clothing should be unrestricted to allow ease of movement and feet kept bare.

6 Read through this book, taking note of the cautions, before you start practising with the DVD.

YOGA PHILOSOPHY

Many people regard yoga as a religion. This is not the case. It is a simple, practical philosophy that does not conflict with, or contradict, any existing religion. As numerous practitioners attest, yoga complements and enriches anyone's personal beliefs. Originally, the teachings were passed on from teacher to student by word of mouth. Somewhere around the 2nd or 3rd centuries BC, a learned sage by the name of Patanjali codified the yoga philosophy into written form.

He stated that:

- The aim of yoga is "stilling the fluctuations of the mind"
- These fluctuations are controlled through consistent practise and detachment (not clinging to the results of the practise, but letting them evolve)
- Enlightenment will result from practising the 8 limbs of yoga

THE 8 LIMBS

1 Restraints in our dealings with the external world (yamas).

2 Observances for our personal self (niyamas).

3 Postures (asana).

4 Breath control (pranayama).

5 Sense withdrawal (pratyahara).

6 Concentration (dharana).

7 Meditation (dhyana).

8 Pure consciousness (samadhi).

The last 6 limbs have been introduced in other sections of this book, so following is a brief description of the first 2 limbs which define the ethics and morals of yoga.

RESTRAINTS (YAMAS)

1 Harmlessness, non-violence – in thought and word as well as deed, basic consideration and respect.

2 Truthfulness, non-lying – to self as well as others.

3 Non-theft – of energy and time, as well as on the material level.

4 Moderation of the senses and appetites – realising the difference between need and indulgence.

5 Non-greed, non-attachment – separating needs from wants, non-possessive, non-selfish.

OBSERVANCES (NIYAMAS)

1 Cleanliness – purity in mind and body, inner and outer.

2 Contentment – acceptance, gratitude, equanimity.

3 Committed focus – integrity of motive, willingness, taking personal responsibility.

4 Self-study – awareness of motives and actions, uplifting readings.

5 Attentiveness to God – whatever you conceive a higher power to be, to nurture your spirit.

These were presented as limbs rather than steps as they can be practised separately or as a whole and in no particular order. It is believed that all humans long for wholeness, unity and completion, so practising one or a few of these limbs will result in integrating all of them in the long run.

Yoga & Breathing

The yoga sages taught that the breath contains prana (life force). By developing the awareness of our natural breath first and then advancing to various control techniques (pranayama), we can enhance and direct the flow and effect of this precious life force.

For example, during the postures if there is discomfort in a certain area, by consciously exhaling into that area we can experience a release of tension making it possible to relax more into the pose.

The breath in yoga is seen as a bridge between the body and the mind and also between the mind and the spirit – the grand unifier.

By focusing on the flow of the breath it can become a tool for concentration (dharana) enabling the mind to develop stillness and one-pointedness (meditation – dhyana). Once this state is reached it is possible for a subtle transformation to occur – a spontaneous feeling of wholeness and union with all that there is (samadhi).

Humming Bee Breath

Bhramari

This simple technique may be used at the beginning or end of your posture work to calm and centre your mind.

Benefits

- Physical – the vibration relieves any blockages and problems of your nasal and ear passages such as sinus and tinnitus, as well as your throat and upper chest, and may also relieve headaches
- Mental – calms and quiets your mind, especially when anxious or unable to sleep
- An excellent preparation for meditation

1 Sit in an easy position where your back is straight with shoulders, face and jaw relaxed. Breathe in and out through your nose at all times.

2 Breathe in normally. Block ears with index fingers. Breathe out and hum. Try to keep your breath even and flowing smoothly.

3 Repeat this a few times and then relax. Observe the stillness and clarity of your mind.

Mountain Pose

Tadasana

Benefits

- Aligns the whole of your body
- Frees up energy blocks
- Allows efficient function of your organs and nervous and circulatory systems
- Allows full flow of your breath
- Corrects poor postural habits

1 Position feet slightly apart, toes facing forward so feet are parallel and in line. Keep your weight evenly distributed over your feet and feel grounded and connected to the earth. Legs are straight without locking into your knees.

2 Take time to align your hips. Top of pelvic rim is level with the floor and hips not tilted too far forward or back. An internal stretch of your tailbone towards the floor lightly firms your lower abdomen. Lift your heart centre, creating space in the centre of your body.

3 Shoulders are broad and relaxed as if placed on a coathanger. Arms and hands are loose and relaxed.

4 Keep your chin level with the floor to avoid compressing your neck. Have a light internal stretch from your heart centre through the crown of your head towards the heavens. Relax your face and allow it to soften. Either close your eyes or soften your gaze.

5 Focus on your breath, the prana (life force) within the breath, and the free-flow of energy.

Important Note

Postures have been shown in this book leading to the left. However for regular practice, it is preferable to start on your right side (refer to DVD).

LIMBERING

ROTATING TWIST

Benefits

- Warms and loosens up your whole body
- Rhythmical movement calms your nervous system
- Activates both hemispheres of your brain creating mental clarity

1 Position feet hip width apart, facing forward and parallel. Keep knees slightly bent.

2 Turn hips from side-to-side allowing your upper body and arms to passively follow the movement. Keep feet firmly planted so you achieve maximum benefit of the movement through your legs.

3 Keep arms and upper body relaxed so the swinging motion releases your shoulders and neck. Keep your head in line with your spine to avoid excess rotation of your neck.

4 Turn your eyes as far to the side as you can – a nice eye exercise. Keep movement going for 30 to 60 seconds.

LIMBERING *(continued)*

ROLL SHOULDERS

1 Slowly roll shoulders up and back on an inbreath. Down and forward on an outbreath.

2 Keep head, neck and body stationary.

3 Reverse the movement, 6 times in each direction.

LOOSEN NECK

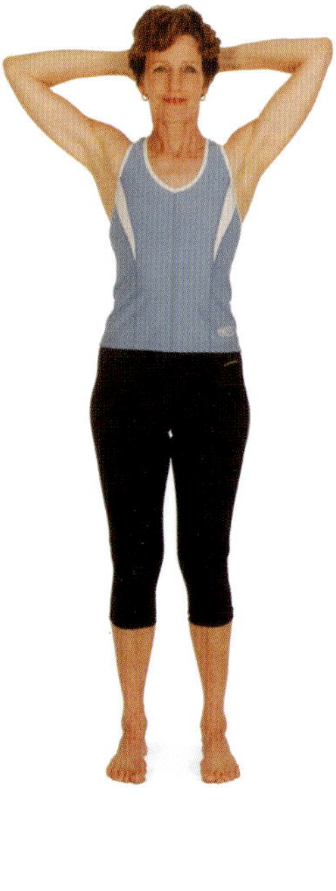

1 Lower head forward and gently shake it from side-to-side. Deepen the movement bringing your chin up towards one shoulder, down to the centre, then back up towards your other shoulder. Hold head forward in the centre. Clasp hands behind your head allowing elbows to fold around your face. Hold for 5 to 6 breaths, allowing the weight of your hands to gently stretch your neck.

2 Breathe in. Return head upright with hands still behind your head. Open elbows out wide. Keep chin low and press the back of your head against your hands. Hold, breathing in and out, then release.

3 Bring one palm to your forehead and press against each other. Hold for a breath and release.

4 Draw shoulders up in a shrug. Gently shake your head from side-to-side, massaging neck against your upper shoulder muscles.

5 Turn head to one side and draw your chin down towards your shoulder. Lift and return back towards your shoulder. Keep shoulders still. Lift head to centre then lower your ear towards your shoulder and shake your head gently as if saying no. Return to centre and repeat on the other side.

LIMBERING *(continued)*

SKI

1 Rock up on your toes, then back on your heels.

2 Use your upper body and arms as if skiing to keep centre of gravity stable. This works all the joints from your toes up through your legs.

SOFTER

If balance is difficult, work each leg alternately. Gradually work up to doing both legs together. Reduce movement of hips and upper body, keeping hands on hips.

Roll Knees

1 Position feet close together and parallel.

2 Bend knees, place hands on legs above your knees and roll knees in circles. Keep your feet flat on the floor. Repeat 5 to 6 times each side.

Roll Hips

1 Bring hands to hips and roll hips slowly and smoothly. Repeat 5 to 6 times in each direction to loosen hips and release lower back.

LIMBERING *(continued)*

CIRCLE OF JOY

For further loosening and warming of shoulders and upper body, and increasing energy flow through your chest.

1 Stand in Tadasana, hands in Namaste (prayer position – page 46).

2 Breathe in. Clasp hands as you breathe out and push your palms away, stretching arms forward with head between your arms and folding forward from your waist. Soften into your knees if you need to.

3 Breathe in. Stretch arms overhead, pressing clasped hands to the sky. Breathe out. Release hands and arms down behind your back.

4 Breathe in. Clasp hands and slowly stretch arms back. Breathe out. Bring arms straight forward palms together. Breathe in. Hands back to your heart. Repeat 3 times.

5 Hold in Namaste for 2 breaths, eyes closed and observing effects.

BEND & STRAIGHTEN LEGS

1 Position legs wide, feet in line and parallel. Bend one leg while stretching the other straight. Alternate from side-to-side.

2 Bend body forward slightly, placing hands and some weight on your bent leg. Keep foot on your straight leg side extended to the outer edge of that foot. Don't lock your knees. Repeat 6 times.

3 Stop movement. Bend knees and curl your body forward. Let head hang to release your neck. Bend elbows, wrap hands around elbows. Let breath flow.

4 Allow release and stretch through length of your back and neck. To come up, keep legs bent, sweep arms forward and up using your shoulders to lift.

SOFTER

If you have blood pressure or heart problems, keep back level with the floor and head in line with, or higher than, your heart. Hands can support on your upper thighs.

SUPPORTED SIDE STRETCH

1 Still with legs wide, extend arms to shoulder height. Breathe in. Breathe out. Tip arms to the left.

2 Rest left hand on your left leg extending right arm overhead and palm facing towards the floor.

3 Hold for 2 breaths. Return upright breathing in. Breathe out and repeat to the right.

Standing Poses

Loosen and relax your body between the postures if you are new to them. Repeat the Rotating Twist or Roll Hips, ensuring a release of any tension.

Triangle Pose

Trikonasana

Benefits

- Strengthens all muscles and joints throughout your body
- Particularly strengthens legs, hips and lower back
- Lateral stretch for muscles supporting spine
- Awakens energy through your organs
- Attention to alignment keeps posture safe and allows freedom of energy flow

1 Position your feet at least 1.5 metres apart, in line and parallel. Lift left toes, swivel on heel and set toes out at 90 degrees to your body. Lift right heel back slightly, approximately 15 degrees. Front heel should be in line with the back instep. Try to keep your right hip back. Always attempt to keep your body in line with your legs.

2 Internally stretch tailbone towards the floor and feel a corresponding firming of your lower abdomen. This activates your pelvic core, providing stability and strength.

3 Stretch arms up level with shoulders. Breathe in. Extend from your heart to your fingertips. Breathe out. Fold from hip over your left leg.

4 Breathe in. Breathe out. Fold forward bringing left hand to the inside of your leg, opening your chest, stretching up with your right arm and both palms facing forward. Breathe evenly as you hold. Build up to holding for a few breaths.

5 Return your body upright on an inbreath. Lower arms and return feet to centre on an outbreath. Repeat on the other side.

Caution

Bend your front leg if you have back problems. If you have shoulder problems align them vertically and allow upper arm to rest behind your back.

Warrior Pose

Virabhadrasana II

Benefits

- Strengthens legs, hips and lower back
- Stretches hip flexors (on the back leg)
- Strengthens quadricep muscles (on front leg, supporting the knee joint)
- Stimulates and tones kidneys and liver
- Fosters mental strength, endurance and confidence

1 Position your feet at least 1.5 metres apart, facing forward and parallel. Hands on hips. Lift left toes, swivel on heel and set toes out at 90 degrees. Lift right heel back to around 15 degrees. Activate your pelvic core as in Triangle Pose. Keep body upright, lifting through your heart.

2 Bend front leg into a lunge, adjusting distance between your feet if necessary. Front knee should be directly above your ankle and in line with your toes. Back leg should be straight and strong with pressure on the outer edge of your back foot. If back leg feels weak, shorten the distance between your feet and reduce the depth of the lunge in your front leg.

3 Raise arms level with your shoulders, keeping a straight line from fingertip to fingertip, palms facing the floor. Look forward over your front hand. Breathe as you hold. Build up to holding for a few breaths.

Archer Pose

1 From Warrior Pose, breathe out and tip back.

2 Bring right hand to rest on your right leg. Breathe in. Stretch left arm forward and up in a straight diagonal line. Hold for 1 or 2 breathes, then return to Warrior Pose.

3 Lower hands to your hips, straighten front leg and turn feet to the front.

4 Repeat Warrior and Archer Poses on the other side.

INTENSE FORWARD STRETCH (BLISS FIX)

PRASARITA PADOTTANASANA

Benefits

- Forward stretch relaxes your back and elongates your spine
- Calms your mind
- Soothes your nervous system
- This version has a stimulating effect on your lymph glands (and other glands), boosts your immune system and ensures production of 'happy hormones'

1 Position your feet at least 1.5 metres apart, facing forward and parallel.

2 Breathe in. Raise arms to shoulder height. Breathe out. Fold from your hips taking your body forward and down.

3 Clasp hands behind your back. Slowly straighten arms back and up taking hands towards the ceiling. Keep your neck relaxed and shoulders away from your ears.

4 To come out of the pose, bend your knees in a semi-squat, thighs strong. Take arms out wide, level with your shoulders. Lift with your shoulders to come up. Roll hips to ensure your body feels at ease.

SOFTER

Bend your knees. Keep arms relaxed on your back. Or, bend your knees and bring hands on to your legs for support, raising back level with the floor and straightening your arms.

BALANCE

With all balances, find a spot in front of you where you can fix a soft gaze, helping your mind to focus.

TREE POSE
VRKSASANA

Benefits
- Provides valuable weight bearing to increase bone mass
- Strengthens muscles and joints
- Improves posture and alignment
- Improves mental focus and concentration

1 Ground firmly through your right foot, gradually taking weight off your left foot. Using your right hand to help, bring your left foot up onto your right leg, foot facing straight down. Aim to bring left heel into your right groin. Employ basic alignments as in Tadasana (page 14), pressing your right leg against your raised foot.

2 When foundation is strong, stretch your arms up overhead, palms together. Aim towards bringing elbows straight, arms a little behind your ears. Hold while breathing deeply and smoothly. Connect your consciousness with the trees – the lungs of the earth.

3 Return hands to prayer position at your heart. Slowly release your left leg. Repeat on the other side. Roll hips to ease hips and lower back.

SOFTER

Stand with back supported against a wall. Only take your raised foot as high as your body allows.

Floor Poses

Cat Pose

Marjarasana

Benefits

- Improves flexibility of your spine
- Relieves tension in your back and neck
- Alternately contracts and stretches abdominal muscles and organs, lungs and heart

1 Position yourself on all fours, knees directly under hips, hands directly under shoulders and arms straight throughout. Breathe in. Stretch tailbone back. Take the stretch through to lift your chest and head. Look straight ahead to avoid compressing your neck.

2 Breathe out as you tuck your tailbone under, arch back up and slowly lower your head. Lead with your tailbone as you breathe in and stretch, then breathe out, curling your back up.

3 Co-ordinate slow smooth movements with slow deep breaths. Repeat 6 times.

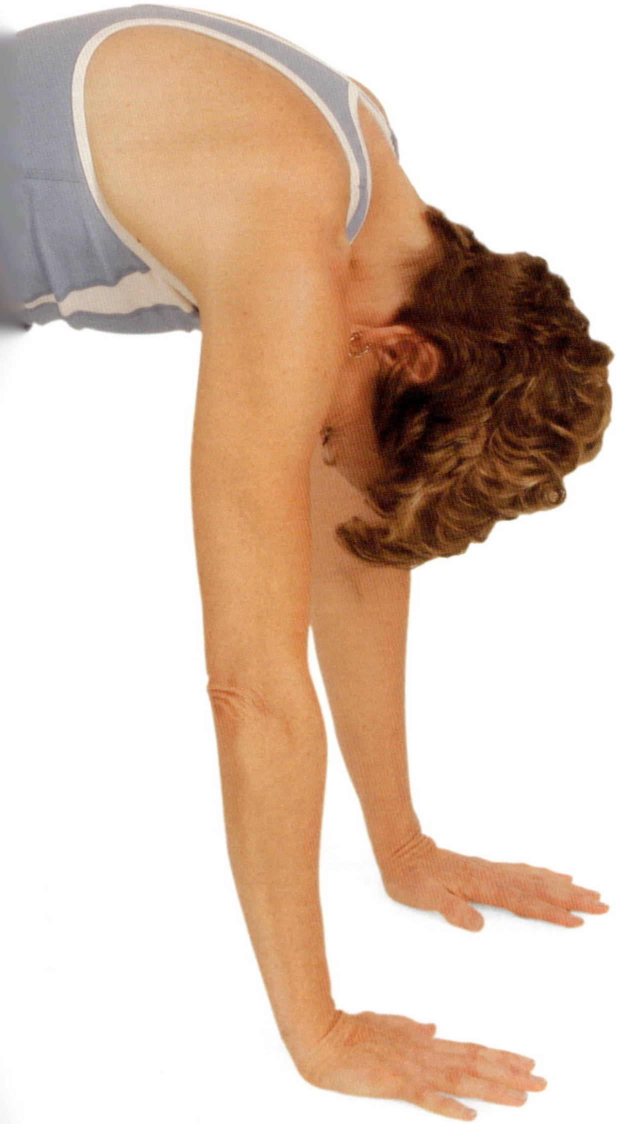

Variation

For a deeper stretch into your lower back.

The inbreath is the same. The outbreath is in 3 parts – tailbone under, bend elbows to the floor, take hips back to your heels.
Repeat 3 times.

Floor Poses *(continued)*

Caution

Do not perform if you have:

- Wrist and/or shoulder injuries
- Eye conditions (glaucoma, detached retina)
- Any disc displacement in your spine
- High blood pressure

Dog Pose

Svanasana

Benefits

- Strengthens all muscles and joints, particularly arms, shoulders and upper body
- Relieves arthritis and fatigue
- It is a part inversion (when you partly turn upside down) with the same rejuvenating benefits to your brain
- Lengthens and strengthens your spine
- Aids organ function and breathing

1 Sit back on heels, feet up on toes. Extend your arms forward, shoulder width apart. Try to align middle fingers with the outer edge of your shoulders. Spread fingers and plant hands firmly on the floor, particularly pressing down on the balls of your fingers so your wrists aren't doing all the work.

2 Press into your toes, moving your hips up and back, stretching your tailbone up. Don't straighten your legs right away if the backs of your legs are tight.

3 Keep neck soft and your head between your arms, looking straight through to your legs. Draw shoulders away from your ears, broaden and flatten across upper back, directing your chest towards your thighs. Avoid dipping into your lower back.

4 If legs allow, slowly straighten directing your heels back towards the floor. Focus on the action through your back first before attending to your legs.

Softer

Keep knees bent. Alternately bend and straighten legs to encourage hamstring muscles to stretch. For weak wrists, roll a towel into a sausage shape and grip your hands over this roll.

3-Legged Dog

For A Challenge

1 Bring feet close together and raise right leg off the floor. Diagonally line up your arms, back and raised leg. Hold for 2 breaths.

2 Return leg to the floor and repeat with your left leg.

CHILD POSE

PRANATASANA

1 Kneel back with buttocks on heels, body resting on thighs, arms alongside your body and forehead resting on the floor. Hold for 1 to 2 minutes.

Improvise with one or more of the following if this is not giving a feeling of ease and release:

- Make a space between your knees to fit your body
- Place a folded blanket or towel between your thighs and calves
- Place a cushion or folded blanket under your forehead
- Bring arms forward, make fists one on top of the other and rest forehead on your fists

Prone Poses

Slide forward to lie on your stomach.

Back Bends

Benefits
- Stimulates and tones kidneys and adrenal glands
- Maintains strength and suppleness of spine and supporting muscles
- Stretches and tones organs and muscles at the front of your body

Caution

Seek advice from your medical practitioner if you have any spinal conditions and/or injuries. Not suitable during pregnancy or if you have a hernia.

Sphinx Pose

1 Stretch arms forward and legs behind.

2 Walk hands back until elbows are under your shoulders, forearms facing forward, upper body gently lifted off the floor.

COBRA POSE

BHUJANGASANA

1 Bring hands under your shoulders, elbows tucked back towards your ribs. Keep thighs actively pressed against the floor, gently stretching back into your feet. Avoid hunching your shoulders.

2 Press hands into the floor and lift upper body from the floor leading with your chest and keeping head in line with your spine. Build up to holding for 3 or more breaths.

CROCODILE POSE

1 To rest, lower body to floor. Bend elbows, placing forearms in front and resting forehead on your arms.

2 Rock hips a little from side-to-side to release any tension in your back. Then lie still and observe your breath.

Reclining Poses

Benefits
- Stabilises your back and hips after the other postures
- Prepares body and mind for inversions and relaxation

Roll On The Back

1 Clasp hands around bent knees and circle your knees slowly a few times in each direction.

2 Make as wide a circle as you can in order to massage a large area of your back. This also calms your mind and nervous system.

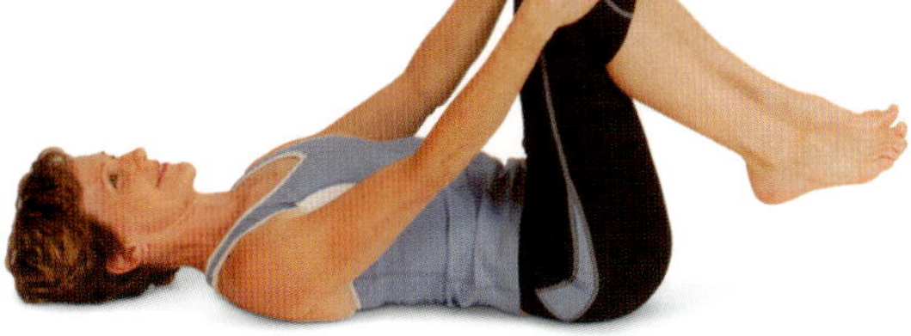

RECLINING POSES *(continued)*

AIRWALK

Benefits
- Strengthens abdominal muscles, particularly your transverse abdominus, while keeping your back safe on the floor
- Using alternate limbs gives a cross-patterning effect on your brain, providing stimulation

SOFTER

Bend knees and don't take limbs all the way to the floor.

1 Stretch your arms and legs up taking hands and feet towards the ceiling.

2 Lower left leg down to the floor while taking right arm back to the floor behind. Return them both back upright as you simultaneously lower your right leg down and your left arm back behind.

3 Keep the movement going smoothly and with an even breath. Only briefly touch the floor before returning. If you rest, it takes more strength to lift your limbs back up.

Hands Around Knees

Apanasana

1 Clasp hands around your knees and rest. Allow knees to press lightly into your arms, keeping your abdominals free, allowing the area to soften with your breath.

Swaying Twist

Benefits

- Keeps spine and supporting muscles aligned, toned and supple
- Stretches muscles and organs in front of your body

2 Release hands, straightening arms up and taking hands towards the ceiling. Knees are bent with feet off the floor. Breathe out. Take legs across to the left and let your arms lower across to the right. Breathe in. Return to the centre.

3 Breathe out. Take legs across to the right and let arms lower across to the left. Keep the swaying movement going slowly and smoothly, co-ordinating your breath.

Softer

Keep arms on the floor out level with your shoulders.

Floating Bridge

Benefits

- Strengthens thighs, buttocks, pelvic floor and abdominals
- Aligns spine, particularly your sacrum and lower back
- Increases flexibility throughout
- The arm movements stretch and release shoulders and upper back

1 Position your feet close to buttocks and hip width apart. Keep feet and knees hip width apart and parallel throughout. Arms alongside your body.

2 On an inbreath, slowly roll your hips off the floor continuing through the length of your back until you have a diagonal line from shoulders up to your knees. At the same time raise your arms up overhead.

3 As you breathe out, slowly roll your back down to the floor returning your arms alongside your body. Synchronise breath and movement. Press feet firmly into the floor to access the strength of your legs.

4 Aim to roll your back, separating your vertebrae, rather than moving it as a single unit. Try 3 to 4 times and build up to 6 times.

Softer

Keep arms on the floor beside your body, or take arms out wide level with your shoulders.

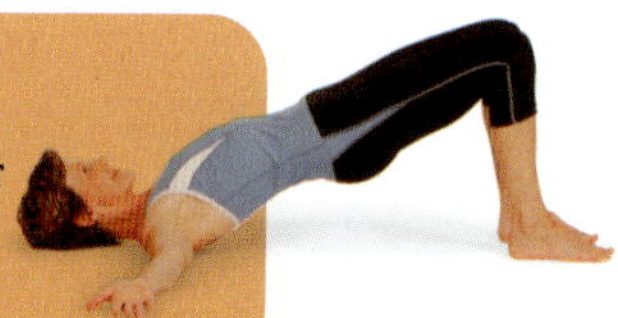

Legs Up The Wall

1 Sit with your body at right angles to a wall. Lean back on your hands and swing your body and legs around, lying down with your legs up the wall and buttocks as close as possible to the wall. Arms rest comfortably at your sides. Stay in position for 3 to 5 minutes.

2 Or, going a little further, bend your knees, pressing feet into the wall and lift buttocks off the floor. Slide bolster or stacked blankets under your sacrum for support. Rest here 3 to 5 minutes. Reverse the process slowly to come down. Once removing the support, lower your back down to the floor.

To return from either version, bend your knees towards your chest. Roll over to the right side and rest briefly before stretching out on the floor for the next pose.

HALF SHOULDERSTAND

Benefits

- Stimulates and tones all your glands, improving hormone function and overall health, wellbeing and immunity
- Reverses the pull of gravity on joints, muscles, organs and circulation – hence its rejuvenating effects
- Relieves fatigue, hemorrhoids, prolapse and varicose veins
- Refreshes your mind and nervous system, providing a sense of clarity
- Strengthens your back and abdominals

1 Once your legs are up, ensure that there is pressure on the centre of the back of your head, NOT on the length of your neck. Your neck remains in its natural curve, chin lower than your forehead and a triangular line of support from the centre of the back of your head along your upper arms to your elbows.

2 Roll back and forth on the floor a few times, taking your legs back overhead until you feel comfortable. Wriggle your shoulder blades closer together, bringing your elbows in close under your body.

3 Raise your legs up, feet above your hips, while lowering your hips onto your hands. If your elbows are not brought in close enough, the weight bearing won't be correct so come down carefully and do Legs Up The Wall. Hold for a few breaths and relax. Try to build up to holding 1 to 3 minutes.

4 To come down, bend knees towards your chest and slowly roll your back down to the floor, keeping hands on your back for support.

CAUTION

This is a safe inversion when done correctly. However, if you have any neck or back problems, eye problems such as detached retina, high blood pressure, heart problems or if menstruating or pregnant, do the softer version (Legs Up The Wall).

Corpse Pose

Savasana

(Refer to the guided relaxation section on the DVD)
Provides complete withdrawal of the senses, relaxing your body and mind while keeping clarity and awareness.

1 Lie on your back, lift head and look to your feet ensuring your head and spine are aligned. Allow your back and neck to settle into their natural curves. Take your legs a little apart so feet can flop, relaxing ankles, knees and hips.

2 Take arms a little away from your body, palms facing up and fingers lightly curled. Shoulders are broad and relaxed.

3 If there is any discomfort in your lower back, place a support (folded blanket or pillow) under your knees. If there is any discomfort in your neck, place a small support under the back of your head. Keep chin low towards your chest.

4 Slowly scan through your body, breathing into and relaxing each part of your body. Then merge with your breath and simply be.

Meditation

Benefits
- Lowers stress levels
- Boosts your body's immune system
- Potential to heal physically, emotionally and mentally
- Calms your mind, giving better clarity, focus and efficiency
- Ability to respond consciously to life's situations rather than reacting from old habits

Due to the ever-changing condition of our work-a-day mind, the meditation experience can alter from day-to-day. Therefore regular practice is the key, and over time we find that our so-called 'monkey mind' becomes more disciplined – at times entering into relative quietness – which enables access to the deeper levels of the mind, levels where we connect with our intuition, creativity and inspiration.

When beginning to practise aim for the same time each day, in a place where you feel relaxed and won't be disturbed. It is preferable to meditate for 5 to 10 minutes daily than for longer periods less often. Meditation is about doing less and 'being' more and retaining awareness in the present moment.

Meditation is the spontaneous progression from concentration to that one-pointed focus where subject and object merge. Your mind is alert but relaxed and open to that blissful state of union with 'all that there is' (Samadhi).

1 Find an object of concentration that suits you personally:
- Watching your breath
- Visualising an image – a beautiful scene, a single object, a spiritual person
- Listening to calming music
- Mentally reciting a mantra

2 As your mind throws thoughts up to the surface of your consciousness, gently bring it back to the object of concentration. It is not about completely blanking your mind but more about letting thoughts flow by without giving them attention. It is like becoming a witness – detaching from the external world, watching but not participating. It does get easier with practise and the benefits are priceless.

3 Sit cross-legged, back straight with shoulders, face and jaw relaxed. Place hands gently in your lap. You may create a mudra (gesture or seal) with your hands to enhance the energy of centredness by joining thumb and index fingertips in a circle, extending your remaining fingers and placing backs of hands on your knees.

4 Close your eyes, relax and focus on the object of concentration.

Partner-Sharing Yoga

Introduction

Partner work can bring an added dimension to the yoga postures. Using the support and assistance of a partner, it is easier to relax and deepen into the stretches. For that very reason, it is important to keep focused and aware in order not to go beyond the limits your body may have at this present time.

Sharing postures with a partner opens your awareness to include another person, adding to the enjoyment and sense of achievement that yoga postures can give. It is ideal to find a partner who is roughly the same height and build and who has similar ability as yourself. However, I have chosen postures where these requirements are not essential. Keep the channels of communication open. Give your partner constant feedback as to how far you want to go and when you are ready to release out of a pose.

If you wish to expand your partner work or have any doubts whatsoever, consult a qualified yoga teacher.

Caution

Take the usual care that you would when practising alone. With any back or joint injuries consult a medical practitioner first and seek guidance from a qualified yoga teacher.

Namaste

(A traditional greeting meaning 'the divinity within me greets the divinity within you')

1 Stand facing your partner with hands in prayer position at your heart centre.

2 Look into each other's eyes and make a connection, silently dedicating this practice to the highest benefit of all.

BACK-TO-BACK SIDE STRETCH

It's a nice warm-up, loosening shoulders and upper back and gently stretching hips, back and side muscles.

1 Standing back-to-back either hold hands or entwine hands around each other's wrists. Try to synchronise your breath.

2 Breath in. Stretch up one pair of arms and on an outbreath, continue moving over to the side keeping the upstretched arms overhead. Keep hips level and upper shoulders back.

3 Hold for a breath or two. Return upright on an inbreath, lowering arms to sides on an outbreath. When ready, repeat on the other side.

4 If you prefer, you could start up a swaying movement, slowly and smoothly taking arms up, over to one side, back upright and down to starting position, alternating sides.

Suspension Bridge

1 Facing each other take hold of your partner's wrists in a monkey grip.

2 Step back until you can fold forward, hinging from your hips and bringing your backs parallel to the floor, a right angle at your hips and your arms straight. Stretch back into your tailbone breathing evenly, keeping your head in line with your spine. Your partner's weight assists your stretch.

3 Broaden across your shoulders opening your chest towards the floor. Try not to hunch your shoulders around your ears. Take time to relax into the stretch.

4 To come out, bend knees slightly and walk towards each other as you come upright.

Partner-Sharing Yoga *(continued)*

Lean back

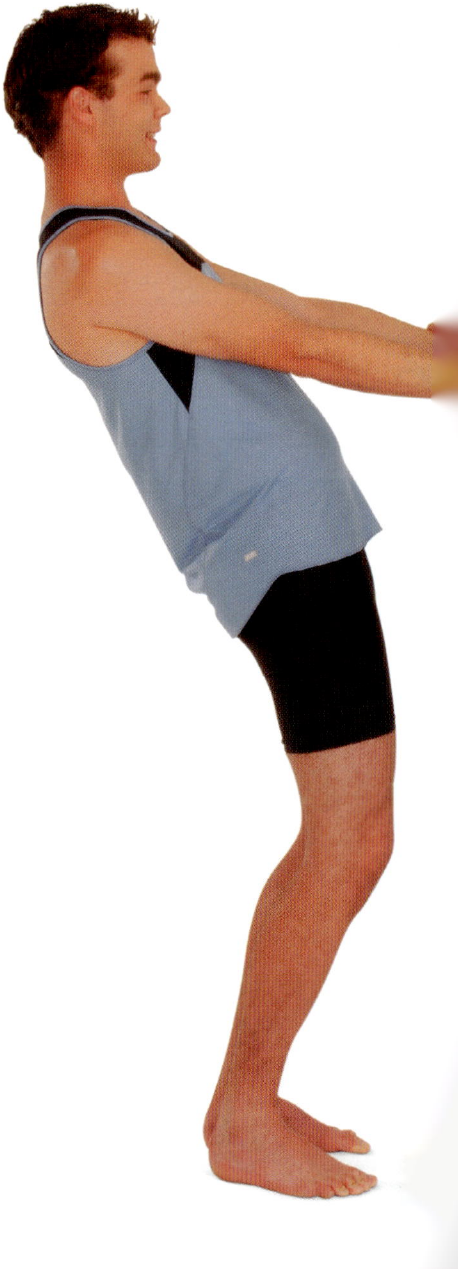

1 Still facing each other with a monkey grip around each other's wrists, come close enough so that your toes are touching. (You may have to adjust this distance according to the length of your arms.) Slowly lean back, straightening into your arms, keeping your bodies straight, shoulders low and tucking your buttocks under.

2 Take time to trust your partner's weight supporting you as you lean back. If, and when, you feel comfortable with your partner's support you could tuck your buttocks in further and arch your back into a backbend.

3 When ready to return, bend your arms bringing elbows back to your body enabling your partner to return upright.

Remember to keep communicating with your partner and indicate if the stretch is too strong and needs to be adjusted, and when you are ready to come out of a pose. Always move slowly with consideration for your partner as well as awareness of your own body.

SQUAT

1 Still facing each other and holding wrists in a monkey grip, step an arms length back.

2 Position feet hip width apart and parallel. Bend knees, connect with the strength in your thighs and the support of your partner's weight.

3 Slowly lower your buttocks to go down into a squat. With the counter-balance of your partner you should be able to keep your heels down, your back straight and shoulders low away from your ears.

4 When ready to come up, lean against your partner's weight as well as using the strength of your thighs.

WARRIOR POSE

VIRABHADRASANA II

Here you will be able to compare how this posture feels with the assistance of a partner after trying it solo in the general class.

1 Face in the opposite direction to your partner and bring the outer edges of your closest feet together. Take hold of your partner's wrist closest to you.

2 Step each of your outer legs into a lunge, making sure that your knee is aligned directly over your ankle and in line with your toes.

3 Keep bodies in line with your legs and extend your outer arms forward at shoulder height. Your partner's weight assists you in staying upright and strong in the pose, making you more aware of the strength in your back leg.

4 To come out, straighten your bent leg, lower arms, turn to the centre and walk your feet together. Repeat the pose on the other side.

Hero Pose

Virabhadrasana I

1 Stand facing each other, step your right foot forward and connect the inner edge of your foot with that of your partner. Step back with your left foot and go into a lunge with your right leg.

2 Keep your hips facing forward and your back leg straight and strong. Don't roll on to the instep of your back foot. If there is any strain to your knee or foot, raise your heel off the floor. Shorten the distance between your feet if you can't keep your back leg strong.

3 Raise arms forward to chest height and press palms against your partner's palms. Try to keep your arms straight and shoulders low. This brings awareness to your upper body, opens your chest and strengthens your upper back. It also helps to balance and stabilise your legs and hips.

PARTNER-SHARING YOGA *(continued)*

SIDE STRETCH

DOUBLE MOON

1 Stand side-by-side about half a metre apart. Hold hands. Breathe in. Stretch your outer arms overhead. Breathe out. Stretch sideways towards each other, bringing your upper hands/fingers to touch.

2 Keep your hips facing forward and upper shoulders back. Hold briefly breathing evenly.

3 Return arms upright on an inbreath, lowering arms to sides on an outbreath. Change sides and repeat.

Tree Pose

Vrksasana

1 Stand closely, side-by-side. Slowly raise your outer foot, using a hand to help if needed. Place your foot against your standing leg and follow directions as described earlier (page 29).

2 Raise your inner arm up overhead and hold your partner's hand (or arm depending on discrepancy in lengths).

3 Raise your outer hand and join with your partner's at heart level in prayer position. After a few breaths, release and change sides.

PARTNER-SHARING YOGA *(continued)*

DOG POSE

SVANASANA

The next three poses are partner-assisted – one performing the posture (**A**) and the other assisting (**B**). **A** performs all three first before changing roles.

1 **A** goes into the Dog Pose as described earlier (page 32). **B** stands squarely behind, bending legs and keeping thighs strong to support back.

2 Place hands around **A**'s upper thighs, apply gentle pressure to guide thighs back encouraging legs to straighten and back and arms to stretch. Listen carefully for feedback so **A** does not over-stretch or hold too long.

3 **A** goes down into Child Pose briefly to rest.

Cobra Pose

Bhujangasana

1 **A** lies prone on the floor arms alongside their body. **B** stands over **A**, feet each side of **A**'s thighs. Note: It is important for **B** to bend their knees and use the strength of their thighs (not the back) for lifting.

2 Grip each other's wrists. On an exhalation from **A**, **B** slowly and smoothly lifts **A**'s upper body from the floor. **A** uses no effort and indicates when they'd like to be lowered back to the floor.

3 If **A** wishes to try Cobra Pose alone (page 36) there could be a pleasant surprise – more lift and ease. **A** then goes into Child Pose.

Partner-Sharing Yoga *(continued)*

Child Pose

Pranatasana

1 **B** kneels alongside **A** and places one hand on their lower back, the other on their upper back.

2 With gentle pressure imagine you are lengthening **A**'s back, lower hand moving towards their tailbone and the upper hand towards their head. You don't have to be heavy-handed to give **A**'s back a nice release and stretch.

Change roles and repeat the last three postures.

SEATED BACK-TO-BACK

1 Either cross-legged or with legs stretched straight in front, lean straight backs against each other.

2 Take a couple of minutes to be aware of your breathing – the slow rhythm. Then bring your awareness to your partner's breath. Maybe your breathing will synchronise, flowing in unison.

PARTNER-SHARING YOGA *(continued)*

BACK-TO-BACK TWIST

1 Cross legs, take your right hand to your own left knee and your left hand to your partner's right knee.

2 Keep backs connected, twist gently and look over your left shoulder. Hold for a few breaths. Release slowly back to centre and repeat to the opposite side.

SIDE STRETCH

1 Place hands together at each side. On an inbreath stretch up one pair of arms. On an outbreath stretch over to the opposite side. Hands on the floor provide support.

2 Keep both pairs of buttocks on the floor and backs connected.

3 Return arms upright breathing in, and back to the floor breathing out. Repeat on the other side.

Facing Twist

1 Turn to face each other, legs crossed and knees touching. Each wrap your left arm behind your waist.

2 Reach forward with your right hand and take hold of your partner's left hand. Twist gently to the left and look over your left shoulder.

3 Keep buttocks firmly on the floor. Release slowly and repeat to the opposite side. (If you don't feel the stretch you could increase the distance between you and your partner's knees but proceed slowly.)

4 As in the beginning, bring hands into prayer position, look into each other's eyes. Bow slightly and thank each other for Sharing Yoga.

Conclusion

My teacher often refers to yoga as "the bridge over troubled waters". Even with the best preparation and control, there are still situations that crop up in our lives that are unpredictable and not necessarily liked.

Yoga has many facets, providing the tools to enable us to ride through the storms of life without being swamped by them. We can practise yoga for the physical benefits alone and can be very satisfied with the results.

However, yoga has the potential to be transformational if we are open to it, replacing old negative patterns with positive, life-affirming choices. I wish you all the clarity, calm and joy that I have found on this journey with yoga.

About The Author

Lynley Woods trained with the International Yoga Teachers' Association (IYTA) and has been teaching in the Sunshine Coast hinterland since 1997. She also instructs in the corporate sector at seminars. Considering herself an ongoing student of yoga, her teacher of 16 years is Elsa Rabold, who was a founding member of the IYTA over 30 years ago.

Elsa is a living example of the benefits of yoga – still practising and teaching at the age of 90. They are both involved in the Sunshine Coast Yoga Teachers' Network – a group of teachers dedicated to furthering the harmony and joy of yoga, as well as the knowledge and experience of its philosophy through regular retreats and workshops.

About The Models

Sarah Burgess lives on the Sunshine Coast and is currently in her second year at university, majoring in nutrition. She has been practising yoga for five years and is convinced of its contribution to a healthy lifestyle. Sarah's interests include health and travel. She feels that overall health and wellbeing will enhance the quality of her life and enable her to live to her full potential.

Matthew Dezoete-Baker lives in Brisbane and works in child care. He wants to expand this work into education and helping children. Apart from yoga, he has trained in tae kwon do and other martial arts. His interests cover a broad spectrum, from football to dancing, health and a wide range of cultural activities. His particular focus is on the Zen philosophy – the discipline of mindfulness.